Islamic Cultures in North America

Patterns of Belief and Devotion of Muslims from Asian Countries in the United States and Canada

E. Allen Richardson

The Pilgrim Press
New York City

This monograph is an excerpt from the forthcoming textbook, *East Comes West: Asian Religions and Cultures in North America*. It is published in advance as a separate monograph in the hope that it might promote understanding in a troubled time to a larger audience than could be reached by the complete textbook.

Library of Congress Cataloging in Publication Data

Richardson, E. Allen, 1947–
   Islamic Cultures in North America

   "An excerpt from the forthcoming textbook, East comes West:
Asian religions and cultures in North America."—Verso t.p.
   Bibliography: p. 59
   Includes index.
   1. Islam—United States. 2. Islam—Canada. I. Title.
BP67.A1R5   297'.0973   81–2876
ISBN 0–8298–0449–8   AACR2

Photographs are by the author except where otherwise indicated.
Illustrations are by William Condron.

The Pilgrim Press, 132 West 31 Street, New York, New York 10001

Contents

Illustrations

Preface

This monograph is concerned with the practice of Islam by Muslims of Asian extraction in North America. The term Asia correctly refers to a diverse body of cultures, including those of the Middle East. This work also recognizes the contribution of other Muslim peoples to the spirit of Islam in America. However, at a time when Muslim cultures in Asia are frequently misunderstood, it hopes to make their particular patterns of belief and devotion that have been brought to North America known.

Acknowledgments

This text was prepared with the suggestions of Dr. Alfreda E. Meyers (Department of Oriental Studies, University of Arizona). Her extensive background in Islamic studies and years of teaching experience were a great asset in developing this monograph. I am also indebted to Dr. Muhammad Abdul-Rauf, former director of the Islamic Center, Washington, D.C., for his helpful comments and advice during the course of the writing.

I am especially grateful to Dr. Paul H. Sherry, Publisher of Pilgrim Press, who enthusiastically supported the production of a text on Islamic cultures in America at a critical time; Mr. Russell Claussen who edited the work and provided numerous suggestions for revision; and Dr. Robert E. Koenig, Editor-in-Chief, whose hard work over a two-year period helped this monograph become a reality.

Finally, I would like to give special thanks to Mr. William Condron who illustrated the text and Mr. J. L. "Woody" Wooden who prepared the photographs that appear in these pages. To these persons and to the *Imams* and Muslim leaders who gave advice and counsel, I am deeply indebted.

E. Allen Richardson

The Islamic Center—Washington, D.C. View of Minaret

Islamic Cultures in North America

An Overview

In the mid-seventh century a revolutionary religious movement swept across the Hijaz, the western border of what is now Saudi Arabia. The charismatic leader of this faith was Muhammad, who was perceived as a prophet and the messenger of God.

Muhammad was an extraordinary leader who achieved a reputation as a statesman, orator, and brilliant strategist. In the face of persecution and open hostility to his religious movement, he is credited with unifying the Arabian people under the banner of Islam. Yet, in spite of these accomplishments, Muhammad could neither read nor write and had little formal education. Orphaned while still a child, he had been raised by an uncle and a grandfather.

After he had married and established a family, Muhammad received the first of a series of revelations that were to continue throughout his lifetime. The record of these revelations later became the Qur'an.[1] Citing Allah (the Arabic word for God) as the source of his visions, Muhammad attracted a small band of followers in Mecca where he had been born. As the revelations grew in intensity and frequency, his circle of supporters expanded.

As the Prophet's popularity increased, opposition also developed. Muhammad had preached a vision of reform in which human affairs were made subordinate to the will of one God, Allah. This was a radical change from the indigenous religion of Arabia, which was a combination of idol worship and animism, in which natural objects were given spiritual or supernatural powers. Muhammad condemned these practices and insisted that, instead of seeking to placate false gods, his followers must submit themselves totally to Allah, the one God. Thus, the faith became known as Islam, which means "submission." Those persons who submitted to Allah were called Muslims.[2]

By A.D. 622, tensions had increased in Mecca, forcing the Prophet to flee. In the company of his supporters, he emigrated to a neighboring city, Medina. This event marks the beginning of the Islamic calendar and is called the *Hijrah*.

In Medina, Muhammad established a model for a society in which Allah was seen as the foundation for a just social order. Each Muslim was required to lead a disciplined life in which five duties were considered authoritative and obligatory. These duties were designated as the Five Pillars of Islam. They included a statement of belief *(shahadah)*, pilgrimage *(Hajj)*, regular prayer *(salat)*, fasting *(sawm)*, and a tithe *(zakat)*, which was distributed among the poor.

The first *Hajj* took place several months before the Prophet's death in 632. Muhammad led a group of Muslims from Medina back to Mecca, which by this time had been recaptured in the name of Islam. The *Hajj* drew its authority from a sacred shrine, a black stone cubicle known as the *Ka'bah*, which according to Muslim tradition had been established by the prophet Abraham. In the course of time, the original purpose of the *Ka'bah* had been forgotten. Instead, it had become a sanctuary for the indigenous religions of Mecca, and a center for the worship of idols. Reaffirming the prophetic monotheism of Abraham and Moses, Muhammad revitalized the worship of Allah and restored the *Ka'bah* to its original use.

The *shahadah* or profession of faith is a creedal statement that defines the identity of a Muslim. It declares: "There is no God but Allah and Muhammad is his messenger." By the sincere repetition of this statement, any person could become a Muslim.

The simplicity of the *shahadah* is an example of the importance of conversion in the Muslim faith. However, the emphasis of the *shahadah* is on the voluntary acceptance of Islam. To accept Islam is to acknowledge the dominant will of Allah and his continuing role of judgment, punishment, and mercy.

Salat or regular prayer is conceived as a precisely controlled act of devotion. It is repeated five times a day at fixed periods of time determined by the position of the sun. The five periods of prayer are: sunset (maghrib), night (isha), dawn (fajr—the time between the dark of night and the actual rising of the sun), noon (zuhr) and afternoon (asr). Before prayer begins, the supplicants wash ritualistically, taking care to cleanse face, hands, and feet. The prayers themselves, like the purification beforehand, are precise. Each prostration or body movement is an act of obeisance. This remarkable homogeneity, with some very minor variation among different schools of Islam, came to symbolize the theological equality of all Muslims. The repeated prostration suggests dramatically that the devotees surrender themselves completely to God. Prayer, the essential act of devotion, affirms the dominance of the divine will and at the same time celebrates the mercy of Allah.

Much like prayer, zakat or almsgiving is highly regulated. As a fixed percentage of income zakat is assessed at one fortieth of each Muslim's annual income. Theologically, it is defined as a loan to God to be distributed among the poor and needy.

Sawm (or fasting), like zakat, is a dramatic symbol of obedience to God. Muslims fast in order to purify their bodies, to become more aware of the holy, and to show humility and abstinence. In the month of Ramadan (the ninth month of the Muslim calendar year), fasting from dawn to sunset is an expected duty of all able adult believers.

Each of the Five Pillars symbolizes the surrender of the Muslim to God and the commitment of the faithful to live in an ordered society in which the will of Allah rules every aspect of human affairs. Although Islam was later to develop its own strain of mysticism called sufism (which has often been perceived as heterodox), the orthodox tradition denied both asceticism and monasticism. Instead of fleeing from the world to find God, the Muslim was disciplined to live in it, continually acknowledging the sovereignty of Allah.

Preaching this revolutionary vision, Muhammad won over most of Arabia by the time of his death. He had fulfilled two roles. Foremost, he was understood to be the culmination or seal of the prophetic tradition that had begun with Abraham. Second, as the very messenger of Allah, he was the source of authority for questions of law and government.

At the time of his death, Muhammad had not designated a successor to continue this second important function. Soon a schism arose over the governance of the faithful. One group of Muslims appointed Abu Bakr, a member of the Quraysh tribe of Muhammad, as Caliph ("successor"). However, a rival faction opposed Abu Bakr and disputed his claim to the office since he was not a blood relative of the Prophet. They supported Ali, Muhammad's son-in-law and cousin. The schism later resulted in the creation of two opposing parties that continue to this day. The majority who selected Abu Bakr as Caliph were known as *Sunni*. The party that supported Ali was called collectively *Shi'a*.[3]

As the rivalry between the two opposing factions increased, violence erupted. Ali was assassinated and his son Hasan poisoned. In 680 under the leadership of Abu Bakr's armies, who tried to crush the dissidents, Ali's second son, Husayn, was killed in battle.

Today, *Shi'i* Muslims view the killing of Husayn as a decisive event in the history of their faith. Husayn is perceived as a martyr and the day of his death is seen as a holy day.

Because of the important position that Ali holds in the Shi'i faith, certain individuals have been designated as his spiritual descendants. These persons, called *Imams*, have been perceived as possessing the power of revelation. Distinctions between *Shi'i* sects have been based on succession to the historical role of *Imam*. Some *Shi'i* (Zaidis) have recognized five Imams while others (Ismailis) have acknowledged seven. Still others (Twelvers) have distinguished twelve. The last has been the official religion of Iran since the sixteenth century.

Shi'i Muslims, however, are a minority in the Islamic world. They are found in Yemen, Lebanon, Iran, Iraq, and Zanzibar as well as parts of India and Pakistan. While *Shi'a* in these and other countries differ with the orthodox *Sunnis* over the question of the *Imam*, the two schools are much alike in other ways. In matters of prayer and theology, distinctions between the traditions are often insignificant.

This monograph describes the perpetuation of both *Shi'i* and *Sunni* forms of the faith among Muslim immigrants in North America. While the adoption of Islam among American converts is beyond the designated purpose of this text, readers are urged to explore it through other sources. Black Muslims—(now designated as Bilalians) are the subject of numerous works that examine the history and growth of the movement.[4]

Several levels of Muslim tradition in North America are described, including ethnic identity, sectarian affiliation and a general adherence to the universal brotherhood of Islam. For example, Pakistani Muslims in the United States often maintain their own mosques and encourage the marriage of devotees within their communities. Similarly, for many U.S. and Canadian Muslims, sectarian affiliation helps instill an important level of personal and corporate identity. Yet, beyond these components of a diversified religious tradition, Islam is also an integrative force that forges common bonds of loyalty to God among different peoples. The text illustrates this cohesive quality of the faith. It shows, for example, how fourteen governments of Muslim countries cooperated to build a multi-million dollar mosque in Washington, D.C. Similarly, in New York City there are plans to construct a $20,000,000 mosque, sponsored by several Middle Eastern countries and U.S. devotees. Such dramatic levels of cooperation between representatives of diverse cultures shows the strength and appeal of the message of the Prophet across thousands of miles.

Islam is a total way of life that affects numerous aspects of belief, daily regimen and culture. In keeping with this level of commitment, Muslim families maintain strong ties with the Islamic culture of which they are a part. Children are brought up in the faith from infancy.

The reader is introduced to one Islamic culture, the Arab-Muslims who maintain strong ties with their homeland. Muslims of Arab extraction have lived and worked in North America for several generations. In some cities, such as Dearborn, Michigan, large communities of Lebanese live in an environment similar to that of their parents and grandparents who first came to this country. Restaurants, coffee houses, grocery stores and other shops enable members of the community to continue important dietary traditions and elements of their culture.

While the history of such communities demonstrates the growth and revitalization of Islam in North America devotees often admit that the practice of their faith here has been difficult. In a non-Muslim environment where many persons are not familiar with Islam, stereotypes and prejudices about the tradition have been a source of hardship for many. For example, during the Iranian revolution in 1979, fear and misunderstanding about Islam were prevalent in the United States. Islamic organizations and mosques became suspect even though in many cases there were few, if any, links with Iran. Some places of worship were desecrated. Distinctions between *Shi'i* and *Sunni* Muslims were frequently distorted or not made clear.

False generalizations about Muslims abound. Islam is often perceived as monolithic and uniform. Such a view not only ignores the cultural differences between Muslims, but dangerously oversimplifies the faith. Whenever isolated groups of Muslim fundamentalists have waged war in the name of the faith, the tradition has been stereotyped as violent. The attack of militants on the Ka'bah in November, 1979 caused reaction throughout the West. The Islamic world was perceived as violent and fanatical even though the vast majority of Muslims were outraged by the attack. While the terrorism was in reality the result of a band of extremists, it became quickly associated with the general character of Islam.

This monograph introduces the student to Islamic cultures in North America with the hope that it will help prevent such misunderstanding in the future. Accordingly, it prepares the reader to encounter the faith with the hope that it will be observed and appreciated, both as an important movement among North Americans who have converted to the faith and in those forms described here.

The Prophet

The most recent major Semitic religious tradition, Islam is a monotheistic religion with a strong doctrine of divine activity in human affairs. It is seen as a human response to God that is guided by a chain of prophetic teachers who are instruments of God's revelation. Accordingly, the tradition includes a succession of many prophets, including Adam, Noah, and Abraham. Jesus is also understood to be a prophet. However, Muslims reject the idea of a son of God (Qur'an-Surah IX. 30) and the crucifixion itself (Surah IV. 157). Since, according to the Islamic view, the unity of God cannot in any way be compromised, there can be no deified Christ and no resurrection. These concepts are looked upon as distortions of the original teachings of Jesus. Further, Muhammad is never seen as divine. Rather, he is the seal of the prophets, the messenger of Allah who, in vision after vision, transmitted divine revelation in the form of the Qur'an.

The teachings of Islam continue the Judaic understanding of a prophet as a social reformer and a teacher of morality. The prophet is understood to act on the authority of God, but not above nor independent of the law of God.

Prophets usually appear in a time of social unrest when the traditional structures of society are breaking down. Muhammad thus began to experience visions when the fabric of Meccan culture was disintegrating. Like much of the Middle East, the nomadic culture surrounding Mecca depended on the existence of clans who upheld the importance of the family and the religious community. But the clan structure in Mecca was deteriorating, while the interests of the dominant mercantile segment of the population prospered.

The popular religion of Mecca was a tradition in which natural objects were given spiritual or supernatural powers. Muhammad's earliest preaching condemned this image worship as being idolatrous. To replace it, he proclaimed obedience to the one God, Allah.

Muhammad followed the usual path of a prophet. He preached the existence of a single God, he condemned popular religious practices that deified objects, and he sought reforms in the social fabric of his day. As his prophetic visions increased in intensity and duration, it became apparent to his supporters that Muhammad spoke with the authority of God. The substance of these visions, which became the Qur'an, were recognized by his followers as of divine origin transmitted to him by the angel Gabriel. Since Muhammad was illiterate, the record of the Qur'an became written evidence of the deity's miraculous intervention in human affairs. Accordingly, Islam has preserved the original language of the revelations, which are understood to be the very words of Allah.

Like the prophets before him, Muhammad's life was filled with dreams and visions that he perceived as emanating from God. These experiences were so powerful that he is reported to have sought solitude away from the bustling commercial city of Mecca. By the time of his Call, Muhammad was a respected businessman who had achieved a good reputation as a trader and commercial agent. He had married a wealthy widow and had raised a family. Yet, those who knew him well must have seen the dramatic evidence of his continuing struggle to understand the visions that often left him exhausted. The effect of these experiences on Muhammad's life was undoubtedly traumatic. At the very point in his career when he had achieved a position of respect and accomplishment secure from economic worry, Muhammad was challenged to accept a new and potentially dangerous role. As the visions increased and Muhammad became even more convinced of his encounter with God, his anxieties accelerated. At the same time he became aware that he had been selected by God as a prophet.

Three incidents in Muhammad's life show how he fulfilled the role of a prophet. The first was a conversion experience on Mount Hira, which is deemed to be his call. According to Muslim tradition, the setting of Muhammad's visions was often the mountains. In Semitic religions, high places usually have symbolized the power and sovereignty of a monotheistic God. Moses, for example, sought God atop Mount Sinai. Muhammad, in a similar manner, sought the solitude of Mount Hira outside Mecca to escape the moral decay of the city below and to seek a place where God could best be approached. It was here that Muhammad first became aware of the deity's direct intervention in his life. The Qur'an records the first verses revealed to Muhammad:

> Recite!
> In the name
> Of the Lord and Cherisher
>   who created—
>
> Created man, out of
> A [mere] clot
> Of congealed blood:
>
> Proclaim! And thy Lord
> Is Most Bountiful—
>
> He Who taught
> [with] the Pen—
>
> Taught man that
> Which he knew not.[5]

The experience of revelation was intense. Muhammad felt compelled to share what he had learned. Though he continued to experience revelations through most of his life, the initial theophany atop Mount Hira remained one of the most powerful of his encounters with the holy. Moreover, his conversion experience was a graphic example of revelation that was in keeping with existing patterns of prophetic tradition. God had spoken, as he had numerous times before in history, through an intermediary who became charged with the transmission of revealed knowledge. In accepting this first revelation, Muhammad assumed the role of prophet who would again and again voice the judgment of Allah. As a reformer, Muhammad acknowledged the unquestioned authority of God. In pronouncing God's decree, he became the instrument of salvation—often at great personal danger.

The second incident that established Muhammad's authority as a prophet was the *Hijrah* in A.D. 622. This emigration was a highly dramatic journey in which the Prophet fled from Mecca to Medina. There, he solidified his support. The event is so important that it marks the beginning of the Muslim calendar.

Though the move to Medina was prompted by the increased hostility of residents of Mecca to Islam, the emigration came to symbolize the acceptance of Muhammad by a growing band of supporters as a messenger of God. Muhammad entered Medina as a victor. Commanding enough support to proclaim the city a center of the faith, he sought to bring Islam to the agricultural peoples of a distant town. The move marked a transition in the manner by which the faith was propagated. Up to this time Muhammad had preached only to members of his own tribe, the Quraysh. Now he broadened his appeal. Uprooting his followers from what had become a hostile environment, the Prophet led his supporters to the oasis of Yathrib. By transforming the oasis into the holy city Medina, Muhammad secured a political and economic base among an economically and socially stable community.

The most visible result of this transformation was the creation of a lasting model of the Islamic state. In Medina, Muhammad created a totally Muslim environment in which all aspects of life were to be governed by God. The city was transformed carefully to bring this about. Even Muhammad's house, set outside the perimeter of Medina, was constructed with a courtyard that could be used for worship. Medina enacted the concept of the Islamic state: there was no division between sacred and secular. The influence of Medina as a model for Islamic society retains its symbolic importance today.

For example, the same model has motivated many of the reforms in the Iranian revolution of 1979. After the fall of the Shah and the establishment of a new government by the Ayatollah Khomeini, elements of western influence in Iran were purged. While reasons for many of these changes are political, they also are religious. The Shah was symbolically identified with the murderers of Ali and his sons, from whom the Shi'a movement is descended. This identification had been noticeable especially on the tenth day of Muharram when Husayn, the son of Ali and grandson of the Prophet, was killed in battle in Karbala in Iraq. Shi'i demonstrators used this day during the revolution to show their hatred for the Shah, and, by virtue of the close association of the Pahlavi government with the United States, their animosity toward America. Such outpourings of emotion were also influenced by the association of the image of the United States with secularism in a country where the

Islamic model of no separation between sacred and secular is an ever-present ideal.

For Shi'i Muslims in Iran, it is logical for an Ayatollah to guide the creation of an Islamic state. The title Ayatollah means "sign of God"[6] and is given to Muslim leaders of high repute and spiritual authority. Each Ayatollah is deemed to be a representative of the Imam. Some Shi'a in Iran identify Ayatollah Khomeini with the word of the Imam so closely that he is seen as the just authority for all questions of law and government.

The values propagated in Medina continue to be normative for Muslims in America. They reflect the cohesion of the Islamic community and the authority of the Imam or religious specialist (which should not be confused with the Shi'i Imamate, the spiritual lineage of Ali). The Imam guides and develops the practical application of the Qur'an to Muslim society. He does not exercise the same function as do Judeo-Christian clergy. Educated in exegesis and theology, he is primarily an interpreter of the Qur'an. In North America, where pressures to conform to the cultural model of a priest or minister can be a source of conflict, the Imam is a unique symbol of the authority of Qur'anic tradition. By his words, he helps devotees to interpret the will of Allah as contained in the Qur'an. His actions are to demonstrate a mode of behavior rooted in submission to God.

Most Imams are highly respected teachers. Frequently, they write tracts on points of doctrine, thus enhancing their traditional role. Some Imams have produced entire courses that help devotees far from mosques or Islamic centers to benefit from their teachings. The Imam also regulates worship. By announcing the call to prayer from a minaret, if the mosque is built in traditional fashion, he reinforces the times and manner of prayer prescribed in the Qur'an.

The third incident in Muhammad's life that dramatized his authority as a prophet was the Hajj or pilgrimage in 632. By 632 the use of the Ka'bah had been fully restored. When Muhammad led supplicants on the Hajj, he dramatized the importance of pilgrimage and affirmed his own role as the spiritual heir of Abraham whose sanctuary he had purified. The Hajj became a duty expected of all Muslims. By praying at the Ka'bah, they reaffirmed their own obedience to Allah and the authority of the one God throughout their lives.

For Muslims in North America or elsewhere, the Hajj remains a most important duty. A devout Muslim plans to make the journey at least once in a lifetime. After making the pilgrimage, supplicants assume the respected title of *Hajji*, which may be prefixed to their names.

The *Hajj* is a powerful experience that is at the very heart of Islam. For Muslims in North America it is a return to the spiritual homeland of their forebearers. Once they have boarded a plane chartered for the *Hajj*, devotees enter a sacred world in which religion affects every action. As a mark of the equality of pilgrims and as a symbol of their purified status, each devotee wears a white, seamless, two-piece garment. During the *Hajj* this garment and the sanctified food that is consumed during the journey symbolize a continued state of purity. The pilgrim lives in a state of *ihram*, or restriction, in which all aspects of behavior are regulated precisely.

Most pilgrims arrive in Jidda, forty-five miles from Mecca (see map, page 19). Once entering Mecca, the supplicant is plunged into a world open only to Muslims. Members of other religious traditions are forbidden from entering the holy ground.

In Mecca, the pilgrim is surrounded by thousands of other devotees from all over the world. Muslims from Africa, the Philippines, Spain, Saudi Arabia, and America converge on this sacred place to take part in a series of rituals. Most perform *tawaf*: walking around the *Ka'bah* seven times. Many yearn to kiss the black stone set in the corner of the *Ka'bah*. The stone is ascribed to Abraham, who is believed to have built the first shrine on the ground where the *Ka'bah* now stands. By performing these ancient rites, the pilgrim reaffirms the authority of Allah in his own life and atones for past misdeeds. The *Hajj* is an act of submission before God. While rooted in the prophetic reforms of Muhammad, it is centered on God's will.

The *Hajj* crystallizes the links between the revelation of Allah contained in the Qur'an, his messenger Muhammad, and each pilgrim. By walking around the *Ka'bah*, by touching the stone laid by Abraham, and by other acts, the pilgrim forges personal ties with tradition. He or she receives support for the only pattern for a devotional life that can exist in Islam—the total submission and commitment to God.

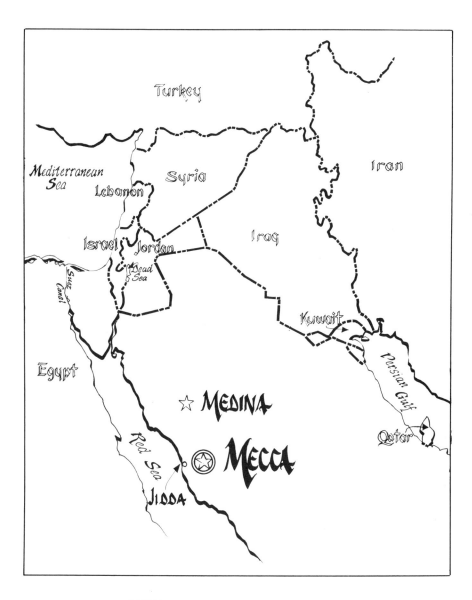

Turkey

Mediterranean
Sea

Syria

Iran

Lebanon

Israel

Jordan

Iraq

Dead
Sea

Suez Canal

Kuwait

Egypt

Persian Gulf

Red Sea

☆ MEDINA

◎ MECCA

Qatar

JIDDA

THE BIRTHPLACE OF ISLAM

Sources of Authority in Islam

Because of its divine origin, the Qur'an is a source of absolute authority in the Muslim tradition. Its significançe for the present is determined through a process of exegesis in which the original meaning of the text is explained. The Qur'an is also a model for questions of law, ethics and social organization.

In addition to the Qur'an, Muslims recognize *hadiths* as a source of authority. A *hadith* is a story about the Prophet. It stresses the dominance of Muhammad's actions, judgments, and opinions in hundreds of different matters. These examples drawn from the Prophet's life are regarded as *Sunna* or direct avenues of authority that have become custom.

The number of *hadiths* is enormous and greatly varied. *Hadiths* can be found for almost every ethical concern or individual act. Each *hadith* is tested for authenticity by a detailed examination of the chain of transmission reaching back to Muhammad. This chain of transmission may be even more important than the content of the *hadith*, since it establishes a dramatic link with the actual words and deeds of Muhammad. Without such verification, the *hadith* loses its authority and becomes subject to speculation.

Islamic jurisprudence or sacred law is interpreted in traditional ways. Muslim jurists recognize several sources of authority—the Qur'an, custom based on an example of the Prophet's life *(sunna)*, consensus *(ijma)* and deductive logic through the use of analogy *(qiyas)*. The last category applies accepted principles of Islamic jurisprudence to new areas of inquiry. There are six major schools of law *(Shari'a)* in Islam, each of which recognizes these sources with differences in emphasis. The six schools are Hanafi, Maliki, Shafi'i, Hanbali, Ja'fari and Zaidi. Each school establishes standards of conduct that affects all aspects of behavior.

In Islamic states, the law is administered by the *ulama*, a prestigeous class of conservative scholars. The *ulama* historically have exercised an important check on the state, upholding the rule of Shari'a law.

Because different schools of Islamic law may recognize different *hadiths*, the obligations and restrictions for individual devotees can vary. This variety has allowed Islam to become strongly adaptable. As a result, the Muslim faith can be practiced in vastly different cultures and has developed different sectarian traditions.

Muslims in North America may belong to any of the six schools of law depending on their country of origin and belief system. For example, the Maliki school often predominates among immigrants from parts of Africa and Egypt, while the Hanafi school is accepted by many Turkish, Indian, and Pakistani Muslims. Each school directly influences the Islamic culture of which it is a part in matters such as marriage, divorce, and patterns of social interaction.

In the United States, as in other non-Muslim countries where the basic institutions of Islamic jurisprudence are absent, there is no *ulama* to administer law or correct actions of the state. In addition, *Shari'a* regulations may conflict with United States civil law. For instance, *Shari'a* law regulates questions of inheritance, prescribing how estates are to be divided among family members. The extended family is often a primary concern in such matters. In countries such as the United States or Canada where civil law predominates over religious concerns, many devotees are caught between the expectations of the family overseas and the legal requirements of the country in which they live.

A Brief History of Muslim Immigrants in North America

In 1933 a New York newspaper reported that a trial had been postponed in order to allow the complainant, an Indian Muslim, to return home so that he might engage in purificatory rites before being sworn in.[7] As a Muslim, the complainant would not take an oath on the Qur'an without first completing a series of rituals, which in his tradition were obligatory.

This brief incident undoubtedly surprised the court officials who witnessed it as well as the public who read of the account. It was unusual because a court of law had temporarily halted its proceedings to allow a Muslim to purify himself before being sworn in with the Qur'an. The court thus sanctioned the substitution of the Qur'an for the Bible and in so doing recognized the complainant's freedom of religion. This was significant since Islam was now formally being recognized as a legitimate religion of a minority group in American society. Moreover, the sanctity of the Qur'an was acknowledged for those who swore on it.

The optimism that this incident sparked was in sharp contrast to the frustration experienced by first generation Muslims who had emigrated from Syria and Lebanon in late nineteenth and early twentieth centuries. These early settlers had little opportunity to nurture or practice their faith. Many were isolated from other Muslims. Most spoke little English and had few personal ties in North America. One early Syrian Muslim, for example, came to the United States in 1902—alone and unsure of where he eventually would settle.[8] He had booked passage on an impulse after seeing many of his friends do the same thing. Coming from an agricultural background, he had few skills that could be used in urban America. He had no choice but to earn his livelihood as a peddler, like many of his countrymen in the same situation. He had no relatives in the United States and had little idea of how to reach other persons from a similar background. He was alone and unprepared. Arriving in the United States, he travelled from New York to Detroit, affiliating in both places with Syrian Christian communities. He found few other Muslims and no community to bolster the traditions he had learned as a child. His plight illustrated the trauma of many other early immigrants who came from the Middle East to America hoping to further their position at a time of economic distress at home. Some Muslims came to the United States at the invitation of sponsors who were a success in business and had come from the same region.[9] These influential patrons helped new arrivals adjust to their surroundings, and often aided them in finding employment and housing. Frequently they became mediators with civic officials. In short, they provided a bridge between the two cultures.

Many immigrants in this early period lost their Islamic identity and were assimilated into American culture. Most found few ways of supporting their religious tradition. The majority of Lebanese and Syrians in the United States were Christian. Thus, Muslim immigrants had little option but to join their countrymen if they wanted the fellowship of persons speaking the same language and understanding the same culture.

By 1914 this early period of assimilation and fragmentation had ended. More Muslims had entered the United States. Islamic organizations in New York and in the Midwest had attracted a growing number of devotees. Muslims in Cedar Rapids, Iowa, for example, had established the beginnings of an Islamic community.[10] Many immigrants were peddlers who later became small shopkeepers, supplying farmers in the area with needed goods. By 1920 the community had established its first mosque by converting a rented hall. In 1929, plans were made for the construction of a formal mosque. An *Imam* was hired to help oversee the effort.

During this early period, Muslims frequently met in small groups for worship and the celebration of major holidays. In Brooklyn, New York in 1925, Muslims met in a room above a Syrian cafe to celebrate the feast that ends the month of Ramadan, a period of fasting. This festival, called *Id al-Fitr* (one of two major festivals abbreviated as *Id*), is a time of great rejoicing in which Muslims may offer special prayers, don new clothes and exchange gifts. A local paper reported that the gathering included persons of different nationalities from the metropolitan area.[11] Such gatherings were significant, since they marked the end of earlier patterns of fragmentation and the establishment of a new unity which transcended ethnic or national identity.

During this time, Arab merchants had settled in different parts of the Midwest and had established communities in Ohio and Indiana. In 1914 an Islamic Center was incorporated as a non-profit organization in Michigan City, Indiana.[12] Members of this community were mostly Syrian and Lebanese who continued the Arab mercantile tradition. Soon the community erected a mosque, which attracted Muslims from three states since no other Islamic centers were nearby.

The Michigan City mosque became a supportive, integrating institution that helped its members express their Muslim identity. The mosque revitalized ethnic and religious traditions, reviving for its members the values and ways of life that they had learned as children. Reflecting its expanding role, the mosque reorganized in 1924 under the name "Asser El Jadeed Arabian Islamic Society." "Asser El Jadeed" meant "The Modern Age." The name affirmed both the Arabic and Islamic heritage of its supporters.

Both the Cedar Rapids (see page 28) and Michigan City mosques began important services to devotees, which continue today. For example, land was obtained for cemeteries (see page 27). This was highly significant since Muslim funerals require burial in a distinctive manner. The corpse is interred without embalming. In most Muslim countries, the body is cleansed, wrapped in a shroud and is interred in a plot that faces Mecca. The eldest sons share the responsibility of the burial.

Muslim cemeteries are usually maintained without elaborate headstones. Theological support for this practice comes from the Islamic injunction that all believers are equal. The only judge of the merit of any individual is Allah who is both merciful and just. Thus, most Muslims reject the use of expensive monuments or mausoleums at the time of death. While this practice has been violated by powerful heads of state and members of the aristocracy in different Muslim cultures, it remains a standard that is often followed today.

The cemetery in Cedar Rapids, Iowa opened in 1948. The six and one-half acre tract met the needs of devotees across the wide geographical area of Iowa, South Dakota, and Indiana. Each plot was carefully surveyed to face Mecca precisely. [13]

The establishment of Islamic cemeteries in the United States was highly significant. It offered Muslims the opportunity to bury their dead in a manner prescribed by their religion rather than the customs of cemeteries run for the use of Jews and Christians. Previously, most Muslims had little choice but to inter their loved ones in plots that rarely faced Mecca in cemeteries that were not designed to meet their needs.

By making possible the continuation of these customs, leaders of the Cedar Rapids and Michigan City mosques were insuring that in life and at the time of death, pervasive elements of Islamic culture would be maintained. This was important since Islam is a total way of life. Earlier Muslim immigrants had experienced a fragmented existence in which dislocated elements of Islamic culture were maintained sporadically. By 1924, with two established mosques providing services to devotees, the beginnings of a more inclusive tradition had taken place.

The traditions begun in Michigan City and Cedar Rapids soon spread to other parts of the country. Gradually, a movement arose to disseminate information about Islam and to organize Muslim communities. By the late twenties, many large cities in the United States and Canada had active Muslim organizations. In New York an *Imam* disseminated tracts on Muslim doctrine to devotees on the East coast. A group of Palestinians and Syrians formed the Young Men's Moslem [sic.] Association. An Arabic newsletter, El-Bayan, kept members of the faith informed of Muslim events and practices. Other Islamic populations in the Midwest and the East followed similar practices.

Where feasible, Muslim societies brought Imams from the Middle East to serve American congregations. The Imam was an important link with the authority of tradition. For instance, the Cedar Rapids mosque hired a prominent Saudi as its Imam who remained there until 1938. Succeeding other religious leaders from different parts of the Middle East, the Imam was an attractive symbol of the vitality of the Cedar Rapids Islamic community. He became a motivating force behind the construction of a new mosque and the perpetuation of lasting traditions.

By the mid-1940s, two events had symbolized dramatically the ability of Muslims in America to establish needed links with Islamic countries, and to develop an increasing sense of cooperation and unity. The planning of the Islamic Center in Washington, D.C. and eight years later in 1952, the birth of the Federation of Islamic Associations in Cedar Rapids, Iowa, marked a major transition for Muslims in America. Muslims had striven to re-establish links with authority and tradition. Now, Islamic communities sought lasting symbols of their identity as fresh arrivals strengthened the tradition in North America.

The birth of the Islamic Center in Washington, D.C.[14] was a highly significant symbol of cooperation between Islamic governments and Muslims in the United States. As the largest, most elaborate project of its kind in North America, the construction of the Center had tremendous significance. It marked the formal acknowledgment of North America as a foreign mission field to which Islamic countries proudly sent their highly trained and skilled personnel.

The construction of the mosque was a symbol of Islamic unity for the fourteen Muslim nations who contributed to the project. Their cooperation upheld the image of the universal brotherhood of Islam. This was significant since the Islamic world historically has been divided by differences in culture, national identity and doctrinal affiliation.

For example, the war between Iraq and Iran in 1980 had roots in the history of Islam.[15] As Islam spread across the fertile crescent in the mid-seventh century, it encountered different cultures. While the inhabitants of present day Iraq (formerly Mesopotamia) were largely Arab, the population of Iran (formerly Persia) was Indo-European. Islam had been brought to Persia in 637 when Arab forces from Mesopotamia were victorious at the battle of Qadisiyah. The battle is still a source of great emotion and has been cited as a reason for revenge in Iran.

The divisions between the two countries were increased by the murder of Husayn, the son of Ali in 680. As the Islamic world separated into Shi'i and Sunni, so the populations of these bordering states adopted different allegiances. Today, Iran is predominantly Shi'i, while Iraq includes both Sunni and Shi'i.

Hence, the early history of the Islamic world, much as that of the Christian church in Europe, has been characterized by idealogical, political and cultural differences. Yet, the utopian ideal of the brotherhood of Islam has always been a persistent goal that has sought to overcome these divisions. The construction of an Islamic Center in the United States with the full cooperation of Muslim governments that have not always been in accord was a powerful symbol of this vision.

The idea for the construction of an Islamic Center in Washington was conceived by an American Muslim businessman and the Egyptian ambassador in 1944. By 1945 the initiative of these two leaders had led to the creation of a Washington Mosque Foundation to secure contributions from Muslims and friends across the United States. After the laying of the cornerstone for the mosque in 1949, the Foundation's executive committee began to assign quotas to the governments of major Muslim countries for underwriting the Center's estimated cost. The effort proved successful. Fourteen governments had contributed funds and gifts in kind to the project by the time it was completed in 1957. In the process, leaders had established avenues of continuing support from the Middle East. The Director's salary, for example, was to be provided on a continuing basis by Egypt. Imams were to be supplied by Al-Azhar University in Cairo, one of the most respected Islamic educational institutions and a source of orthodoxy and theological authority.

Muslim National Cemetery—Cedar Rapids, Iowa

The Islamic Center and Mosque—Cedar Rapids, Iowa

Every detail of the Islamic Center was planned strictly according to tradition. Located on a 30,000 square foot tract of land, the minaret, the marble columns, and the archways of the mosque conform to precise standards of Islamic architecture, replicating the finest patterns of construction.

The Islamic Center was an unprecedented venture that marked an increased level of religious cooperation amongst Muslim countries in support of a U.S. mission. The Center became a symbol of Muslim unity and identity in the United States and the emergence of Islam as a major American religious tradition. It continues to support an Islamic consciousness among the various Muslim communities in the United States.

The formation of the Federation of Islamic Associations (F.I.A.) in 1952 continued the efforts of the Washington Mosque Foundation to broaden the image of the United States as the home of a significant Muslim population. It also marked a heightened level of cooperation among U.S. Muslims who now supported a truly North American federation.

The F.I.A. was conceived by an American soldier in World War II. Abdallah Igram had been incensed when he discovered that the armed forces did not recognize the designation "Muslim."[16] Further, no reference to Islam could be inscribed on dog-tags. After his discharge in 1945, Igram returned to his home in Cedar Rapids, Iowa, determined to help end such examples of discrimination. He began working toward the realization of a new dream—the establishment of a society for Muslims that would unify the voice of Islam in North America. The response to Igram's dream was overwhelming. More than 400 Muslims met in Cedar Rapids in 1952 and formed the International Muslim Society. A year later in Toledo, Ohio, a second convention attracted more than 1,000 persons. In 1954 in Chicago the organization adopted a constitution and a new name, "Federation of Islamic Associations in the United States and Canada." Abdallah Igram had served as the president of the International Muslim Society and its successor, the F.I.A., until 1955. His dream had become a reality. The F.I.A. emerged as a coordinating body that sought to promote a greater cohesiveness between U.S. and Canadian Muslims.

The F.I.A. interested the government of Egypt in its efforts when, soon after the organization's formation, two F.I.A. officials met with the head of state, Gamal Abdel Nasser. He contributed $50,000 toward a new mosque in Detroit. They also secured the pledge of the services of four *Imams* who would come to the United States.

This event was highly significant for several reasons. First, it firmly established the ability of Muslim immigrants to transcend regionalism and to look beyond their individual mosques and communities. Second, it demonstrated the ability of Muslims in America to perpetuate the authority of the foremost Muslim University, Al-Azhar, strengthening the formal ties with orthodox Islamic tradition. Through these efforts, the Muslim community in America secured an avenue for the regular revitalization and enrichment of its practices.

The formation of the F.I.A. with its ability to gather Muslims from all over the United States and Canada into cooperative ventures, helped pave the way for other North American Islamic organizations. One of the most significant of such recent organizations is the Muslim Student's Association. With headquarters outside Indianapolis, Indiana, the M.S.A. is a coordinating agency for graduate and undergraduate Muslim students on campuses across the United States and Canada. With the sharp increase in America of students from Arab countries, South Asia, and other parts of the Muslim world, the M.S.A. served a large body of students who later chose to remain in the United States after the completion of their education. The increase of these persons in the United States was dramatically aided by the reforms in immigration laws in 1965 and the elimination of the national origins quota system. Some have married American citizens and entered a wide range of professions and occupations. This new population is highly skilled and well-educated. The Muslim Students' Association, drawing on these resources, has established numerous programs that often reach beyond the campus. For example, the M.S.A. supports an Islamic Press, which distributes publications among its member associations. Many of the publications help the M.S.A.'s members—the majority of whom have been in North America less than six years—to continue their religious traditions. The M.S.A. helps fresh arrivals to practice their faith in a non-Muslim environment and, if they wish, to prepare for a lasting residence in the United States and Canada.

In order to realize these goals, the M.S.A. has developed a highly refined and efficient organizational structure. The agency is divided into zones that include the western, central and eastern parts of the United States plus Canada. Each zone is divided into regions under the administrative supervision of regional directors. Zones hold regular council meetings and offer sponsor conferences on varying points of Muslim doctrine and practice.

The Muslim Students' Association was formed in response to the need for Islamic organizations directed at specific Muslim populations. Today the Islamic Medical Association, the Moslem [sic] Social Scientists and Moslem [sic] Scientists and Engineers are examples of this type of federation. They are professional groups who are concerned with a theological correlation between occupation and religious beliefs. Such professional groups are able to lobby vigorously on behalf of their Muslim members and to help counteract misconceptions and prejudices about Islam.

Another coordinating agency, The Council of Muslim Communities of Canada, was formed in 1972. The Council succeeded a smaller, more regional organization—the Ontario Council of Muslim Communities. By 1977 the body included forty Islamic associations and mosques throughout Ontario, Newfoundland, Quebec, British Columbia, Alberta, Saskatchewan, and Manitoba. The Council promotes Islamic education in Canada and sponsors youth camps, conferences, and exchanges, as well as a variety of public relations programs.

Each of these organizations has established supportive relationships with the seats of Islamic orthodoxy and authority in the Middle East. For example, the Federation of Islamic Associations maintains close relationships with the Rabita in Mecca, the World Muslim Congress in Karachi, the Supreme Council for Islamic Affairs in Cairo, and other groups. The F.I.A. and other organizations frequently interact with such important domestic organizations such as the Council of Imams. The latter furthers cooperation among mosques in North America and is an association of Muslim spiritual leaders. The theological importance of the Council is contained in its careful preservation of the role of the Imam as a source of authority and tradition.

⟨Thus, in little more than sixty-five years, Muslims in North America have generated a strong community identity.⟩Islamic associations and mosques exist in almost every state. Maintaining strong support relationship with the seats of Islamic learning and government in the Middle East, the community takes pride in its diversified ethnic and cultural heritage, but at the same time acknowledges a common monotheistic tradition. Nonetheless, both *Shi'i* and *Sunni* forms of Islam are practiced in America. But doctrinal identification is usually not a source of conflict or division where all Muslims are members of a minority. Recent studies have demonstrated that in communities where Shi'i and Sunni mosques exist, the affirmation of one's identity as a Muslim is a unifying thread. For example, in Dearborn, Michigan, where members of the Zaidi Shi'i sect and Sunni Muslims have emigrated from different parts of Yemen, sectarian differences are recognized but they do not disrupt the community.[17] Both Shi'i and Sunni Yemenese participate in a Yemeni Benevolent Association, they have intermarried, and marriage partners frequently stress the fact that both are Muslim rather than emphasize doctrinal differences. This attitude reflects a change from Muslim countries, where such patterns of intermarriage are infrequent.

Membership in religious groups may also be a source of great pride. Near Edmonton, Alberta, for example, a Druze community replicates customs and patterns of social relationships found in a Lebanese village. The reconstruction of these important traditions is so complete that according to one researcher there were few real differences between this Canadian community and the one in Lebanon, except for a change in dress.[18] These Druze, like those in the Middle East, acknowledge the messianic leadership of an eleventh century Caliph, al-Hakim, who is recognized as an Imam in the Shi'a tradition. The Druze faith draws its name from al-Danazi, who spread early doctrines of the faith. As other Shi'i movements, it is based on hidden revelation and the strong cohesion of the worshiping community. The Druze tradition, however, is regarded by many to be outside the orbit of Islam.

Similarly, for members of the Pakistani Ahmadiyya movement, the community is a source of great strength. Based on the teachings of Hazrat Ahmad, a nineteenth century religious leader, Ahmadiyya devotees recognize a succession of teachers who are direct descendants of the founder. Supplicants regard these men as successors to the Mahdi or messiah (Hazrat Ahmad) and as continuous sources of divine revelation. For this reason the movement is regarded as heretical and outside the theological boundaries of orthodox Islam by Sunni devotees, who see Muhammad as the seal of the prophetic tradition. Yet, members of the Ahmadiyya movement identify themselves as Muslims.

As early as 1920, an Ahmadiyya mission was opened in Chicago in an attempt to spread the faith to America. Subsequently, in 1923, 1925 and 1928, additional missionaries were sent to the United States.

Through the efforts of these and later religious leaders, mosques were eventually established in Chicago, New York, Pittsburgh, St. Louis, Dayton, and Washington, D.C. Other missions have been established in Milwaukee, Wisconsin; Philadelphia, Pennsylvania; Teaneck, New Jersey; Waukegan, Illinois; and Baltimore, Maryland. Twenty-six chapters or *jamaats* are now active in the United States. In addition, four have been established in Canada. Each chapter is responsible to the Director General of the Ahmadiyya Muslim Foreign Missions office in Pakistan.

The missionary efforts of the Ahmadiyyas reflect the importance of conversion in Muslim related traditions. Based on the teachings of Muhammad, who perceived the need for the rapid transmission of the faith, Muslims continue to advocate their faith. Conversion, however, must be voluntary; as such it is an acknowledgment of the total sovereignty of Allah.

In conclusion, Muslim sects and reformist movements depend on the re-establishment of traditions transported from great distances. A Druze community in Edmonton, Alberta, achieves this end by reconstituting social relationships and important customs in Canada exactly as they were done in Lebanon. In much the same way, Ahmadiyya groups in major U.S. and Canadian cities forge links between leaders of the movement in Pakistan and devotees in North America. In each case, Islamic movements offer the devotee a chance to continue customs of belief, law, ritual and patterns of social relationships begun overseas.

Opening Ceremony of the Dayton Ahmadiyya Mosque—September 4, 1965   Courtesy: The American Fazl Mosque, Washington, D.C.

The Mosque in North America

In a large two story building in a residential section of San Francisco, members of a Muslim community worship together every Friday. Downstairs, there are classes in Qur'anic exegesis while the upstairs loft has been converted into a room for prayer. There, sheets have been placed on the floor so that the sanctuary will remain pure. Devotees enter the prayer room without shoes, having washed in the kitchen below. They pray facing a large window in the direction of Mecca, while a leader of the community begins the call to prayer.

This scenario is repeated in mosques across the United States and Canada. Each mosque varies in manner of construction and appearance. Some, such as the Islamic Center and Mosque in Cedar Rapids, are modern while incorporating distinctive architectural conventions from the Middle East, such as the dome. Others, as in a Tucson, Arizona mosque are entirely functional and are built in part of a home. Still others, such as Masjid Al-Arkam in Worchester, Massachusetts, have been erected in converted churches. A few, however, fully replicate distinctive patterns of architecture and decoration found in Muslim countries. The Islamic Center in Washington, D.C., for instance, combines elements of Muslim art from many different nations.

Decorations in mosques such as the Islamic Center are confined to calligraphy and geometric designs. Islam forbids any art that depicts the human figure including that of the Prophet Muhammad. Any art that risks establishing idols or ascribing substitutes for God (a sin called shirk) is intolerable to all schools of Islam. Passages from the Qur'an may be inscribed inside as a reminder for the faithful that the mosque is the house of God. The photograph on page 39 shows an example of the intricacy of design and detail as incorporated inside the Islamic Center in Washington, D.C.

The sanctuary of a mosque is covered by carpets. There can be no chairs, pews, or other obstructions that might hinder the movements and acts of prostration that are part of prayer. Instead, the emptiness contributes to a strong sense of tranquility. Thus, even in the midst of a worshiping community, the devotee can be alone with God. Moreover, in the carpeted interior of the mosque, all devotees are completely equal and on the same level.

Unlike most churches, mosques are not built for lengthy processions or for the display of choirs or large organs. Except for the *minbar* or pulpit used by the *Imam* to address the assembled community, the sanctuary gives the feeling both of open space and of intimacy. A large open chamber may be interspersed with ornate pillars that permit devotees to seek Allah corporately, yet privately, in a defined space.

Symbolic of their role in the Islamic community, many U.S. and Canadian mosques are constructed to facilitate large assemblies of devotees. Muslim holidays such as New Year's Day (the first day of the lunar month of Muharram), the Prophet's birthday, and the beginning and end of the fast period of Ramadan are festive occasions that draw large crowds. At these times, the community may gather in anterooms of the mosque to celebrate the event.

Regardless of their appearance, mosques in·America fulfill several important functions. Foremost, they are houses of prayer, with prayer rooms or sanctuaries that face Mecca as directly as possible. When the sanctuary is in a building designed originally for another purpose, the prayer room is arranged so that devotees face Mecca. By facing Mecca, supplicants are reminded regularly of the origins of their faith. Whenever regular prayer is observed on Friday the worshiper acknowledges the prophetic traditions of Abraham and Muhammad, and the importance of Mecca.

The mosque is also a center of Muslim education. In some cases, Islamic leaders have arranged Sunday school programs at a time convenient for a western, urbanized society. In many Muslim Sunday schools, language studies and theological issues are of prime importance. The mosque is a place where Arabic is taught. Second, third, and even fourth generation Arab Americans, Pakistanis, Indonesians, and other Islamic peoples are given the opportunity to learn the language of the tradition.

Many mosques have installed Islamic libraries to encourage the theological education of its supporters. One of the primary purposes of the Islamic Center in Washington, D.C., for example, was the construction of a place where regular Islamic research could be conducted. Smaller mosques throughout the United States and Canada offer similar services. For example, a mosque in Tucson, Arizona, maintains a collection of Islamic newsletters and publications, offering supplicants a chance to maintain essential ties with other U.S. Muslim communities.

Mosques and Islamic centers frequently publish newsletters to attract new members and promote activities of the center, and inform devotees of programs in other centers. Whether a newsletter promotes the construction of a new mosque or the study of the Qur'an, Muslims have found it an effective way to maintain contact.

The educational function of the mosque is perhaps best dramatized by a feat that was recorded in the Cedar Rapids Gazette in 1936.[19] Two boys, seven and twelve years old, had achieved a reading knowledge of the Qur'an. For Muslims throughout the Midwest, the event held great significance. It demonstrated that in America the mosque could continue to function as the predominant means of educating children in the tradition. A reading knowledge of the Qur'an is a highly valued part of the faith, because it enables devotees to exegete the text in its original language. No translation of the Qur'an can be authoritative. A knowledge of Arabic is essential if the text is to be read in the same form as that revealed to Muhammad.

Muslim education is influenced by *da'wah*, the preaching of the Prophet's message. *Da'wah* is considered by many U.S. and Canadian Muslims as an integral part of all religious instruction, and essential for the success of adult education programs.

Some mosques have been able to maintain their educational programs without the services of an *Imam*. Under such conditions, members share regular duties and leadership. For example, a mosque in Toledo, Ohio, in 1960 was administered by a board of trustees. Six or seven lay preachers shared the responsibility of the Friday homily. Even without the benefit of a full time *Imam*, the mosque maintained a strong educational program that included classes for children.

Mosques in North America may include large numbers of particular ethnic segments of the Muslim community, such as Lebanese in Dearborn, Michigan, Pakistanis in New Jersey or Bilalians in Brooklyn, New York. The worshiping community is a source of solidarity for each ethnic group. For instance, a group of Syrian and Lebanese immigrants erected a mosque in Cedar Rapids, Iowa, in 1934. Except for its dome, the building had little in common with the elaborate mosques in the immigrants' homeland. The walls were made of wood instead of stone. Instead of graceful lines the features of the sanctuary were plain. However, the significance of the mosque was not its method of construction or appearance. Rather, for that small group of Muslims, it was a powerful, physical symbol of the perpetuation of their faith and way of life in America.

Because mosques are such important symbols of the continuity of Islam in America, Muslim groups have worked hard to erect them. Frequently they have found opposition from persons outside of the tradition. For example, when a band of twenty families sought to erect a school and religious center in New Jersey's Hunterdon County, they encountered hostility from local residents. The Pakistanis requested a zoning variance that would allow the structure to be built. The community reacted out of fear and clearly did not understand Islam. A meeting of the local board of adjustment to decide the matter was the largest ever held in the area. As emotions surged, the issue became linked to questions of patriotism. A newspaper account reported, "The crowd was so large . . . that the engines in the firehouse had to be moved outside to accommodate the turnout. Many of those attending had been attracted by anonymous flyers, embossed with an American flag, that were distributed earlier and which urged that the township's zoning laws be upheld."[20]

The Islamic Center—Washington, D.C. Frontal View

Regardless of their ethnic heritage, all Muslims in America are members of a minority by virtue of their faith. While most have experienced misunderstandings about their religion, they usually find support in the regular gatherings of the worshiping community. For instance, a second generation Arab American living in the Midwest commented that throughout his life he had been forced to explain and defend his faith to peers and associates. Some had little idea who Muhammad was and few realized that Muslims, like Christians or Jews, share a Semitic heritage in which the worship of a single God is paramount. In the mosque this man was able to talk with persons of similar backgrounds who also had experienced these frustrations.

Similarly, Muslim communities foster the continuation of traditional values. The importance of keeping the traditions is stressed to teenagers: They are urged to abstain from alcohol, avoid dating, unlike non-Muslim peers, and marry according to the wishes of parents who will secure a suitable mate. In the interim, to offset what otherwise would be a very isolated life among persons who do not understand Islam, the mosque offers the companionship of other devotees who share a common worldview.

The mosque is thus the heart of the Islamic community in North America. It is a symbol of Muslim identity in an environment that often has not understood Islam and has been hostile to it. Whether it is constructed in the best architectural traditions of the Middle East, or in the home of a resident *Imam*, a mosque is an extension of the spirit and devotion of each unique Muslim community.

Arab Muslim Culture

The Muslim world is culturally diverse. Islam is widely practiced in parts of South, Southeast and East Asia as well as Europe, Africa and the Middle East. In each Muslim society, Islam directly affects patterns of diet, dress and interpersonal relations.

The history of Islamic peoples in North America reflects this diversity. Muslims in North America include persons from such distant places as India, the Philippines, Iran, Arab countries as well as indigenous Americans who have converted to the faith. This section is focused on one of the largest populations of immigrant Islamic peoples, Arab Muslims, who have actively practiced their faith here for over seventy years.

As members of a religious minority in the United States and an ethnic minority, Muslims from Arab countries living in North America have been subjected to misrepresentations about their culture and religion. Many Americans have little understanding of what an Arab is and often accept popular images of nomadic bedouin as the norm. In reality, the Arab world consists of a variety of Christian and Muslim peoples in: Saudi Arabia, Yemen, Democratic Yemen, Oman, the United Arab Emirates, Qatar, Bahrain, Kuwait, Iraq, Jordan, Syria, Egypt, Libya, Morocco, Tunisia, Algeria, southwest Iran, and parts of southern Turkey. There is no single "Arab" identity or way of life. Rather, the term correctly refers to a diverse group of people who share a regional identification and linguistic, political and historical bonds. By far the greatest unifying force in the Arab world has been Islam. Under the banner of Islam the Arab civilization achieved its greatest triumph and formed distinctive patterns of science, art, architecture, law and government.

In America, Arab peoples have been subjected to persistent stereotypes that ignore both the diversity and depth of this civilization. In film, newspapers, and other media, Arabs have been described in romantic terms based on popular perceptions of bedouin and nomads.

For over half a century, Americans have had a love affair with adventure films set in the Arabian desert. Since the days of Rudolph Valentino *The Sheik* (1921) and Douglas Fairbanks *The Thief of Bhagdad* (1924), the allure of swashbuckling romance and battle in the desert sands has stirred the imagination of moviegoers.

However, this genre of films has been marked by pervasive stereotypes about Arabs and Islam. Arab peoples have consistently been portrayed as the warlike inhabitants of a barren wasteland whose only inhabitants are bedouin and camels. Films such as *Beau Geste* (Ronald Coleman, 1927) portrayed an Arab horde of four thousand who without mercy attacked forty Legionnaires.[21] The movie was an epic of its day, but sacrificed accuracy in the interest of drama. Like other films in the genre, it was made thousands of miles from any Arab country, in this case, in Arizona. Other films used romantic images of Arabs to evoke fantasy. The Middle East was seen as a land of mystical beasts, magic carpets and an ever present medievalism.

Sanctuary, Albanian Islamic Center—Harperwoods, Michigan
Courtesy: *Imam Vehbi Ismail, Albanian Islamic Center*

It is this last association of Islam and the Arab world with medieval imagery that continues to this day. Many Americans view Islamic society as primitive and opposed to all forms of progress. It is still dominated by such stereotypes as the "law of the desert" in which water is seen as more precious than human life. In the movie *Lawrence of Arabia* (Peter O'Toole, 1962), this was the underlying motive behind the murder of a tribesman who sought to steal water from a well. Such characterizations continue to portray Arab peoples as barbarian. A group of Canadian Muslims protesting this symbolism recently spoke out against a cartoon that depicted the early Arab Muslims as a plundering horde. Similarly, Arab Muslims voiced objections to the designation ABSCAM, asserting that it defamed their image.[22]

ISLAMIC CENTER
OF MICHIGAN CITY

Rudolph Valentino and Agnes Ayres in The Sheik (1921). The film catapulted Valentino into stardom and simultaneously popularized the stereotype of Arabs as barbarian adventurers who lived by the same moral code as pirates or outlaws. In the film a young English woman (Agnes Ayres) plans a trip into the Arabian desert against the will of her family. She is captured by a Sheik (Rudolph Valentino) who carries her off to his desert lair where they eventually fall in love.

Rudolph Valentino and Vilma Banky in Son of the Sheik (1926). This film extended both Valentino's popularity and the image of Arabs as hot blooded soldiers of fortune. Like Beau Geste and other desert films to follow, it was filmed in Yuma, Arizona.
(Photo courtesy of Killiam Shows, Inc.)

In addition, since rising gasoline prices became a source of public frustration and anger, persons from the Middle East have been stereotyped as wealthy. The perception of the ruthless bedouin hordes popularized in film, has been augmented with an image of affluence. For the majority of Arab Americans who come from modest backgrounds, this understanding is a source of great uneasiness. On college campuses with large international student bodies, it has often resulted in prejudice and discrimination.

The Middle East has remained an enigma to most Americans. Textbooks rarely provide an accurate understanding of either the relevance of the Middle East in world history or the presence of Arab peoples in the United States. In *Scratches On Our Minds: American Images of China and India,*[23] Harold Isaacs suggests that many Americans remain uncertain about the term "Asia" or such regional disignations as "Far East" or "Middle East." He concludes that this confusion among school children, in particular, has been increased by the use of maps which have a geographical center the longitude of Peoria, Illinois.[24] These charts, which have replaced the older Mercator projection, divide Asia into distorted masses. On such maps designations of the "Far" or "Middle" East have little relevance to the actual location of countries.

These misunderstandings about the Arab world persist even though some Arab neighborhoods have existed in North America for over sixty years. In Michigan, for instance, a third generation Arab American community is still dominated by the ever-present coffee house, Syrian restaurant, and grocery stores, suggesting continuity in dietary laws and social relationships among immigrants.[25] Such neighborhoods, showing varying degrees of traditionalism, are found across the United States and Canada. In New York, for instance, grocery stores specializing in Middle Eastern foods are a common sight along Brooklyn's Atlantic Avenue. The small shops are often dramatic evidence of the extended family in America. They may be managed by family members who employ nieces, nephews, and even distant cousins who are all treated as important members of the household.

For thousands of Arab Muslims, Islam is a unifying thread that reinforces a strong sense of identity. Islamic concepts of marriage and the extended family, the community and such basic traditions as diet, have helped many Saudi Arabian, Lebanese, Syrian, Palestinian, and Yemenese groups retain their cohesiveness.

A particularly cohesive city is Dearborn, Michigan where there is the greatest concentration of Arab Americans in the United States, 95% of which are Muslim.[26] There a Lebanese village has been reconstituted in the midst of an urbanized, industrial area. As many as six hundred members from the same village live within five blocks of one another.[27] In this tightly knit community, many persons are related, and live together much as their parents and grandparents did in Lebanon.

For this highly traditional Muslim society in the United States as for others, marriage is an important institution. Most members prefer to marry within their culture and religion. Many children grow up expecting to live in the same neighborhood and practicing a lifestyle similar to that of their parents.

Qur'anic tradition suggests that Muslim men may marry members of other Semitic religions, including Jews and Christians. But, since Arab culture perpetuates a strong patriarchal tradition, the assumption is made in such marriages that any children will be brought up in the faith of their father.

Marriage rites in America are often performed by an *Imam*. According to *Shari'a* law this is not necessary, however. Any qualified Muslim who is familiar with the tradition can perform a marriage. In many Islamic countries a village registrar is responsible for conducting the rite.

However, since clergy in America usually perform marriages, many *Imams* follow the convention and do likewise. Some Sikh *Granthis* in the United States have accepted the same role. *Granthis* are highly respected Sikhs who read the Guru Granth Sahib before assemblies of devotees. The Guru Granth Sahib is the one text in the Sikh tradition regarded as sacred scripture. However, neither the *Granthi* nor the *Imam* are perceived as clergy within their respective traditions. Instead, they are religious specialists with specific tasks that frequently differ from those of ministers or priests. For example, *Imams* are respected Muslims and scholars who are responsible for leading the faithful in prayer. They are symbols of Islamic values and provide a model for other Muslims to follow. *Imams* do not exercise a pastoral role as a minister is expected to do. Indeed, there is no office of pastor in Islam and the symbolism of a shepherd is not applied to leaders of the faith.

In America, when *Imams* have been stereotyped as clergy, they have experienced difficulty in maintaining their traditional roles. They may be expected to perform some of the duties of a pastor and at the same time uphold the orthodox Islamic values of the faith they represent. Most *Imams* are particularly sensitive about this issue, which can be a source of tension and frustration.

Islamic associations and mosques play an important part in sustaining the marriage. Large gatherings of Muslim families reinforce the dominant values of the tradition, bringing persons of similar backgrounds together. Through the association of different families, bonds are forged that frequently culminate in marriage. Moreover, as in Muslim countries, these ties have economic as well as religious and social importance.

Among orthodox Muslims, the tradition of the dowry is usually continued in North America. The dowry is an example of how the extended family takes part in the marriage process. Frequently, the husband gives his wife *mahr*. This is a gift that symbolizes the marriage contract. The marriage may be formalized in a document known as the *nikkahnama*, in which the arrangements for the dowry and *mahr* are made. The *nikkahnama* is a cross-cultural concept of great significance. It can determine the division of the estate after a divorce, (which in Islamic law is considered binding if declared by the man three separate times). Frequently, after a divorce, the *mahr* (often including jewelry) is the property of the bride. It establishes a form of security for the woman while at the same time regulating the separate but independent worlds of husband and wife.

In the *Purdah* system, common in Muslim countries, men and women move in different worlds. The role of the female is inside. She is the guardian of the home and the family. By tradition, she is forbidden from entering the outside world of her husband. By the same token, she has absolute rule at home. In South Asia, as a mark of her status, she may wear the *burka*, a cloak that shrouds the body and covers the head. The *burka* allows the inside world of which she is an integral part to be transported intact. It also reinforces cultural standards of modesty and propriety.

In America, the use of garments such as the *burka* is impractical. Vestiges of the *Purdah* system, however, do survive among the more traditional families. In Dearborn, Michigan, for example, Lebanese women often continue the same pattern of life as in the Middle East. They safeguard the home and important family traditions. They do not frequent coffee houses, which are the traditional domain of the men. Yet they maintain a dominant role in the education of their children into the tradition and the perpetration of the faith in the family. The use of large sunglasses, or clothes that cover the wrists and ankles may serve a function similar to the *burka*. As Muslim women keep traditions of modesty and propriety and maintain their accustomed role in the home, *Purdah* survives, though in a less visible form.

The role of the Muslim woman is powerful in her own realm. She is responsible for the continuation of dietary laws, for education, and for a variety of social networks that are integral to the culture of which she is a part. In many Muslim societies she may be a cousin of her husband. This helps to assure that the extended family will function as an economic unit.

However, the role of Muslim women in America can also be filled with frustration and confusion. While many second and third generation Muslim families have assimilated into American life, newer arrivals often have not. Wives may be expected to conform to customary standards of dress and behavior that are difficult to maintain in the United States. They may know few other Muslim women and feel alone and alienated from the American culture of which they are now a part. Similarly, they may be discouraged from holding a job or planning a career and instead be expected to remain in the home.

For single women additional conflicts may arise. Muslim women frequently do not date. Because of Islamic prohibitions on music and dancing they may be unable to accompany their friends to school functions. The rejection of these common elements of American life cause many to be misunderstood and to face enormous conflicts.

The problem is compounded for American women who marry Muslim immigrants. They are often expected to conform to the world of their husband and to adopt his way of life. For those wives who are unfamiliar with Islam or Muslim culture, the resultant problems are enormous when the freedom they have always expected is threatened by the values of their husbands. However, despite these hardships and conflicts, many couples have been able to work out a satisfactory accord.

However, the wife in these instances may also be an important factor in helping her family to assimilate into life in the United States. A study among Syrian and Lebanese Muslims in Chicago showed that in such cases a large percentage of women work and, in fact, are a primary means through which traditional patterns of family life in the Middle East are broken.[28] In such instances, the customary patriarchial role of the male is weakened as the family adapts to a new economic situation in which both spouses contribute to the combined income.

The matter of diet presents other complications in North America. Traditionally, Muslims may not consume liquor or pork, nor eat meat that is not slaughtered in keeping with Islamic law. These dietary obligations are kept in obedience to Allah and as a way of supporting a high level of ritualistic purity. Unless a Muslim is pure, he cannot engage in regular prayer or read from the Qur'an. Hence, great care is taken to avoid sources of contamination.

In Arab Muslim communities, dietary restrictions are maintained carefully. Problems may arise, however, for school children or for those in any institution unfamiliar with Islamic traditions. One Dearborn school solved these problems by providing a protein diet for Muslim children whenever pork was served in a school lunch.[29] In other communities with large populations of Muslims, butchers sell meat slaughtered in the proper fashion.

For Arab Muslims in America, language is another important element of culture and religion. Children born in America often are bilingual. Many families speak Arabic at home and want to raise children in the language of their parents or grandparents.

Recently, there has been a strong movement among Islamic communities to provide formal language instruction. A private school in Philadelphia, for example, specializes in Arabic education for children. Some Islamic associations also offer courses in Arabic and a variety of Islamic presses in the United States provide correspondence courses.

The proliferation of Islamic publishers shows the evolving strength of the Muslim community to provide for the continuing education of its members. Contrary to the popular impression of Islam, such organizations rarely proselytize and usually seek their market among persons already within the faith. The presses also reflect the economic strength of the Arab Muslim community in North America. Many professional persons have invested their time and savings in such ventures.

The ability to understand written Arabic has immense theological importance. As noted earlier, it enables the believer to read the Qur'an in its original language and to interact with a source of scriptural authority that cannot be understood through translation. Further, knowledge of the spoken language helps children to absorb the traditions of their parents. It is a link with both religion and culture and a continuing source of pride.

Maintaining traditions of marriage and the extended family, diet and language is crucial to this diversified population of Muslims. They are aided by increasing numbers who have entered the United States since 1965 when immigration laws were changed radically. A growing number of students from Arab countries have been educated at American colleges and universities. Many marry and remain. Becoming leaders of Islamic societies and mosques, these devotees help nurture patterns of prayer and diet, and encourage the retention of Arabic. These new immigrants often assist others in understanding difficult verses or patterns of language in Qur'anic study. They are important sources for renewing the religion and culture of their predecessors.

Also, the generations of Arab Muslims have made significant contributions to the total life of the United States and Canada. Many have excelled as engineers, scientists and doctors.[30] They have retained pride in their Middle Eastern heritage while at the same time been productive citizens of the communities of which they are a part.

Renewal and Adaptation in Muslim Communities in North America

In 1978, a New York newspaper reported that a coalition of Islamic countries had agreed to help finance a twenty-million dollar mosque on the city's upper east side.[31] The complex included a school, an exhibit hall, and a library, which were incorporated in a sweeping modern structure that included distinctive elements of Islamic architecture. A minaret in the futuristic design complemented the vertical thrust of the New York skyline. The article suggested that the idea for the mosque had been supported for ten years by three Arab states—Saudi Arabia, Kuwait, and Libya—who had put up seed money for the project. Now, with contributions from the United Arab Emirates, Malaysia, Iraq, Iran, Jordan, and Morocco, and with the continuing contribution of services of an *Imam* from Egypt, they could begin.

This project is part of an evolving tradition in North America in which links with Muslim leaders and heads of state or religious leaders in the Middle East have been forged repeatedly. Following a pattern begun in the thirties, when *Imams* were brought to Iowa from the Middle

East, the undertaking reflects the same motivations that led to the building of the Islamic Center in Washington in 1957.

Established mosques with long histories of activity in North America continue much the same tradition, inviting important religious leaders from the Middle East to visit their communities. They accept the invitations because of a continuing concern of Muslim countries for devotees in the United States and Canada. These leaders are important symbols of renewal. Their presence helps reaffirm basic values and re-establishes ties with the Semitic origins of the faith. Such visits also help to perpetuate the Islamic community in North America.

Often among recent immigrants, links are maintained faithfully with family members who remain in Muslim countries. The continued nurturing of Muslims in America in the faith is a matter of deep concern for relatives abroad. Parents maintain an active role in the perpetuation of cultural traditions that are important links with Islam. The extended family is often a primary concern. Even distant cousins are highly valued. Such close ties with family members overseas provide a support system for relatives who come to North America.

Further, since the mosque is the most visible symbol of the community's identity, devotees go to great lengths to establish mosques that can perform several functions. The mosque is a place where entire families meet for regular worship and for major festivals. It may be a multi-purpose structure constructed so that devotees can congregate for Qur'anic exegesis. Often, it includes a place for common meals and gatherings.

Mosques in America may resemble their Middle Eastern counterparts. Or, they may be entirely functional, adapting a home or church for purposes of worship and study. Such adaptations show the ability of Muslims in America to practice their faith, using available resources to the best possible advantage. The theological requirements of a mosque, however, are met once the site has been purified and the proper direction for prayer established.

The erection of mosques in America also is a way of spreading the prophet's message (da'wah). In an effort to overcome prevalent stereotypes about Islam, groups like the Council of Muslim Communities in Canada have established Public Relations divisions to provide accurate representation of the tradition.

Da'wah may also include the distribution of informative literature and the establishment of Islamic presses. Devotees in Cedar Rapids, Iowa, for instance, help support a press that publishes information about the faith in English. This service is particularly important for third or fourth generation Muslims who may have little knowledge of Arabic.

Similarly, some Muslim associations have developed their own curricula supplemented with linguistic aids for persons not fluent in Arabic, courses in the language itself, and texts on Islamic theology and doctrine. These materials, written by leaders of the tradition and hence considered authoritative, are part of an ongoing process of Muslim revitalization. Moreover, their sheer abundance demonstrates the economic solidarity of the Muslim community and its willingness to invest time and resources.

As educational institutions, mosques adapt traditional functions of the *madrasa* or Islamic school. In the Ottoman Empire, the *madrasa* was an important component of the mosque where *Shari'a* law was learned, jurists trained and teachers educated. Often subsidized by the state, the *madrasa* provided for the continued assimilation of children into the tradition.

In the United States or Canada, the functions of the *madrasa* may be met in a variety of ways. The community may establish a library or an Islamic School. The sketch on page 56 demonstrates the practical applications of this concept used to plan a Muslim Community Center in Silver Spring, Maryland. A mosque, two classroom buildings, a library and administration building are included.

Muslims in North America frequently experience conflict when Islamic teachings are contrary to the basic institutions of American life. For instance, the concept of paying or receiving interest is against Islamic law. In North America where interest payments or credit cards affect every sphere of economic activity, the devout Muslim who seeks to live in accordance with *Shari'a* law faces major conflicts.

Almsgiving *(zakat)* can also be problematical for Muslims in America. In Islamic countries *zakat* may be collected by the state or community. In North America, similar arrangements are clearly impossible. Yet, for all Muslims, the payment of *zakat* is an expected duty. In order to help alleviate this dilemma, some Islamic groups have adapted the tradition in innovative ways. Leaders of the MCC project in Silver Spring, Maryland urge their benefactors to consider donations to the center as *zakat*. The construction of this large complex that will meet the needs of large numbers of Muslims is looked upon as charity.

There also are conflicts experienced when differences of opinion become issues between generations. For example, one of the most emotional issues in Islam is music, which has been a source of scholarly debate since the first Muslim century.[32] The debate centers on the propriety of music and dance in an Islamic society. Since in Muslim theology there can be no distinction between sacred and secular, the question of the legitimacy of musical expression is not a matter of its association with religion. Rather, any type of music can be a source of dissension. However, most Muslims agree that musical forms associated with sensuality are forbidden.

In America, the dissension on this issue is frequently intergenerational. Muslim children feel enormous peer pressure to join their friends at dances, rock concerts or social gatherings in which music is a part. For high school students in particular, family restrictions that forbid going to the senior prom or a school dance can be a source of immense frustration. Further, the popularity of music throughout American youth culture, makes the conflict difficult to ignore. For parents, however, who still have family members in Muslim countries where *Shari'a* law is predominant, the assimilation of their children into American culture can be quite threatening. In addition, the periodic visit of Muslim dignitaries to Islamic societies in the United States increases the pressures to conform to accepted standards of behavior.

The issue is compounded by the fact that many non-Muslim Americans have been exposed to Islamic culture and have little sympathy with restrictions they do not understand. Accounts of Islam in the newspaper or radio may be distorted or taken out of context. For example, during the Iranian revolution (1979-1980), the media reported that music had been banned. On popular television programs, this became a matter of ridicule. By implication, the humor reinforced existing stereotypes of Islam as antithetical to the modern world and virtually medieval. The long-standing debate on the subject within the Islamic world was ignored.

Thus, we have seen how, for almost three quarters of a century, Muslims have nurtured their faith in North America. At first fragmented and with few methods of revitalizing basic traditions, many Muslims were unable to find ways of sustaining their culture or beliefs. In less than fifty years, however, community leaders have re-created a dynamic base. Constructing mosques, opening Islamic schools, and establishing links with sources of authority in the Middle East, they call the faithful back to God:

> And He is God: there is
> No God but He. To Him
> Be praise, at the first
> And at the last:
> For Him is the Command,
> And to Him shall ye
> (All) be brought back.
>
> Qur'an,[33]
> Surah xxviii:70

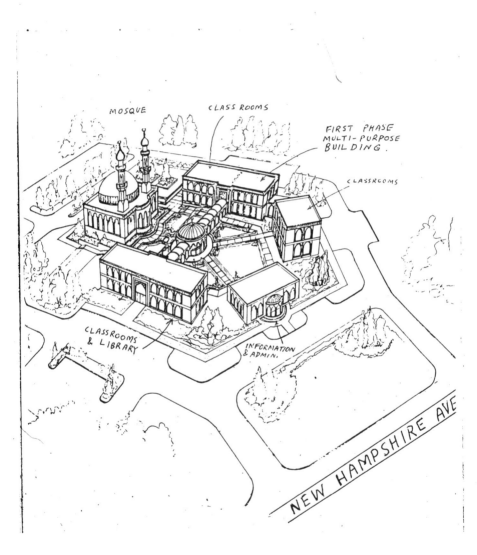

Muslim Community Center—Silver Spring, Maryland
Courtesy: Abdul Rauf, M.D. Editor, MCC Bulletin and Member of the
Board

Notes

1. The spelling "Qur'an" is preferred over the more Anglicized "Koran" by the majority of Muslims.
2. The designation "Muslim" is preferred over "Moslem." The term "Mohammaden" is offensive and should not be used.
3. The singular form of the noun "Shi'a" is "Shi'i."
4. See, for example, Charles Eric Lincoln, *The Black Muslims in America*, Revised Edition (Boston: Beacon Press, 1973) and Malcolm Little, *The Autobiography of Malcolm X* (New York: Grove Press, 1965).
5. The passage has been adapted from: *The Holy Qur'an, Text, Translation and Commentary*, Abdullah Yusuf Ali (Washington: The Islamic Center, 1978), Surah 96: 1–5, pp. 1761–1762.
6. *Newsletter of the Task Force on Christian-Muslim Relations. A Project of the Commission on Faith and Order of the National Council of the Churches of Christ in the U.S.A., in cooperation with the Duncan Black Macdonald Center for the Study of Islam and Christian-Muslim Relations, The Hartford Seminary Foundation*, No. 8, April, 1980.
7. This incident was originally reported in the *New York Tribune* and later received attention in *The Moslem World*.
8. Abdo A. Elkholy, *The Arab Moslems in the United States* (New Haven: College and University Press, 1966), p. 121.
9. Nasseer H. Aruri, "The Arab-American Community of Springfield, Massachusetts" in Elaine C. Hagopian and Ann Paden ed., *The Arab-Americans: Studies in Assimilation* (Wilmette, Illinois: The Medina University Press International, 1969), p. 51.
10. Philip Harsham, "Islam in Iowa," *Aramco World Magazine*, November-December, 1978, p. 34.
11. H. I. Katibah, "Moslems of City Celebrating Pious Feast of Ramazan," [*sic.*] *Brooklyn Eagle*, April 18, 1925. Quoted in Beverlee Turner Mehdi, ed., *The Arabs in America, 1492–1977: A Chronology and Fact Book* (Dobbs Ferry, N.Y.: Oceana Publications, Inc., 1978), p. 81.
12. "Islam in Michigan City, Past and Present" (Michigan City: Islamic Center, n.d.).
13. Yahya Aossey, Jr., "Fifty Years of Islam in Iowa 1925–1975" (Cedar Rapids, Iowa: Unity Publishing Co., n.d.).
14. See, Muhammad Abdul-Rauf, *History of the Islamic Center* (Washington, D.C.: Islamic Center, 1978).
15. A. O. Sulzberger, Jr. "Roots of War in the Gulf," *New York Times*, September 24, 1980, sec. A, p. 10.
16. Umhau Wolf "The Islamic Federation, 1952: 'Muslims in the American Mid-West,'" in *The Muslim World*, L, January 1960, 42–43. Quoted in Beverlee Turner Mehdi, ed., *The Arabs in America, 1492–1977: A Chronol-*

ogy and Fact Book, p. 103. See also in the same volume (p. 111), Jay Walz "Nasser Donates to U.S. Moslems: Two Midwesterners Fulfill Mission in Cairo—Imams Will Be Sent to Teach," *New York Times*, September 20, 1959, p. 21.

17. Barbara C. Aswad, "The Southeast Dearborn Arab Community Struggles for Survival Against Urban 'Renewal,'" in Barbara C. Aswad, ed., *Arabic Speaking Communities in American Cities* (New York: Center for Migration Studies, 1974), pp. 53–83.

18. Louise E. Sweet, "Reconstituting a Lebanese Village Society in a Canadian City," in Aswad, ed., *Arabic Speaking Communities*, (New York, 1974), p. 50.

19. "Boys Master the Koran in Arabic" *Cedar Rapids Gazette*, January 12, 1936. Quoted in Mehdi, ed., *The Arabs in America*, p. 93.

20. Ronald Sullivan, "A Moslem School Upsets Hunterdon," *New York Times*, May 21, 1978, sec. xi , p. 20.

21. James Robert Parish and Don E. Stanke, *The Swashbucklers* (New Rochelle, N.Y.: Arlington House, 1976), p. 118.

22. Accounts of correspondence between the F.B.I. and Muslim community and religious leaders regarding the ABSCAM designation appear in spring 1980 editions of the *Muslim Star* (Detroit, Michigan: The Federation of Islamic Associations).

23. Harold R. Isaacs, *Scratches On Our Minds: American Images of China and India* (New York, N.Y.: John Day Company, 1958).

24. Ibid., p. 40.

25. Laurel D. Wigle, "An Arab Muslim Community in Michigan," in Barbara C. Aswad, ed., *Arabic Speaking Communities*, pp. 155–167.

26. *Newsletter of the Task Force on Christian-Muslim Relations*, April, 1980.

27. Aswad, "The Southeast Dearborn Arab Community," p. 62.

28. Safia F. Haddad, "The Women's Role in Socialization of Syrian-Americans in Chicago," in Hagopian and Paden, ed. *The Arab Americans: Studies in Assimilation*, pp. 84–101.

29. Aswad, "The Southeast Dearborn Arab Community," p. 64.

30. One of the most well known Arab Americans is Dr. Michael A. Shadid who organized the first cooperative hospital in the United States in 1929. Dr. Shadid is recognized as a pioneer in the field of cooperative medicine.

31. Youssef M. Ibrahim, "'Showplace' Mosque Planned on East Side." *New York Times*, July 26, 1978, sec. B., p. 1.

32. For a summary of this debate see, A. Shiloah, "The Dimension of Sound; Islamic Music—Philosophy, Theory and Practice" in Bernard Lewis, ed., *Islam and the Arab World; Faith, People, Culture* (New York, N.Y.: Alfred A. Knopf in association with American Heritage Publishing Co., Inc., 1976), pp. 161–180.

33. *The Holy Qur'an, Text, Translation and Commentary*, Abdullah Yusuf Ali, p. 1021.

Select Bibliography

Abdul-Rauf, Muhammad. *History of the Islamic Center.* Washington, D.C.: Islamic Center, 1978.

_____*The Life and Teachings of the Prophet Muhammad.* London: Longmans, 1965.

_____"Pilgrimage to Mecca." *National Geographic,* 153, No. 11 (November 1978), 581–207.

Aossey, Yahya Jr. *Fifty Years of Islam in Iowa 1925–1975.* Cedar Rapids, Iowa: Unity Publishing Company, 1975.

"Arabs: A Clash of Cultures" (three articles). *Arizona Daily Star* (Tucson), May 27, 1979, sec. B, p. 1.

Aramco World Magazine. Published bi-monthly by the Arabian American Oil Company, New York, New York.

Aruri, Nasseer H. "The Arab-American Community of Springfield Massachusetts." In *The Arab-Americans: Studies in Assimilation,* pp. 50–66. Edited by Elaine C. Hagopian and Ann Paden. Wilmette, Illinois: The Medina University Press International, 1969.

Aswad, Barbara C., ed. *Arabic Speaking Communities in American Cities.* New York: Center for Migration Studies, 1974.

_____"The Southeast Dearborn Arab Community Struggles for Survival Against Urban 'Renewal.'" In *Arabic Speaking Communities in American Cities,* pp. 53–79. Edited by Barbara C. Aswad. New York: Center for Migration Studies, 1974.

Atiyeh, George N., ed. *Arab and American Cultures.* Washington, D.C.: American Enterprise Institute for Public Policy Research, 1977.

Berger, Monroe. "Americans from the Arab World." In *The World of Islam,* pp. 351–372. Edited by James Kritzeck and R. Bayly Winder. New York: St. Martin's Press, 1959.

Brockelmann, Carl. *History of the Islamic Peoples.* New York: Capricorn Books, 1960.

"Boys Master the Koran in Arabic." *Cedar Rapids Gazette,* January 12, 1936. In *The Arabs in America, 1492–1977 A Chronology and Fact Book,* p. 93. Edited by Beverlee Turner Mehdi. Dobbs Ferry, New York: Oceana Publications, Inc., 1978.

Chirri, Jswad Imam Mohammad. "The Five Daily Prayers." Detroit: Islamic Center of Detroit, n.d.

Cragg, Kenneth. *The House of Islam.* Encino, California: Dickenson Publishing Company (Religious Life of Man Series), 1975.

Elkholy, Abdo A. *The Arab Moslems in the United States Religion and Assimilation.* New Haven: College and University Press, 1966.

Gibb, H.A.R. *Mohamedanism.* New York: Oxford University Press, 1971.

Gotje, Helmut. *The Qur'an and its Exegesis; Selected Texts With Classical and Modern Muslim Interpretations.* London: Routledge and Kegan Paul, 1971.

Guillaume, Alfred. *Islam.* Revised Edition. Baltimore: Penguin Books, 1956.

Haddad, Safia F. "The Women's Role in Socialization of Syrian-Americans in Chicago." In *The Arab Americans: Studies in Assimilation* pp. 84–101. Edited by Elaine C. Hagopian and Ann Paden. Wilmette, Illinois: The Medina University Press, 1969.

Hagopian, Elaine C., and Paden, Ann. *The Arab-Americans: Studies in Assimilation*. Wilmette, Illinois: The Medina University Press International, 1969.

Haiek, Joseph R., ed. and publisher. *The American-Arabic Speaking Community Almanac*. Published annually by The News Circle, Los Angeles, California.

Hardy, P. *The Muslims of British India*. Cambridge: Cambridge University Press, 1972.

Harsham, Philip. "Islam in Iowa." *Aramco World Magazine*, 26, No. 6 (November-December 1978), 30–36.

Hitti, Philip Khuri. *Islam, A Way of Life*. Minneapolis: University of Minnesota Press, 1970.

_____*The Syrians in America*. New York: George H. Doran Company, 1924.

The Holy Qur'an, Text, Translation and Commentary. Abdullah Yusuf Ali. Washington, D.C.: The Islamic Center, 1978.

Ibrahim, Youssef M. " 'Showplace' Mosque Planned on East Side." *New York Times*, July 26, 1978, sec. B, p. 1.

Isaacs, Harold R. *Scratches on our Minds: American Images of China and India*. New York: John Day Company, 1958. Revised edition, M.E. Sharpe, Inc., 1980.

The Islamic Center. *Essentials of Muslim Prayer*. Washington, D.C., n.d.

_____"Islam and Muslims in North America." Washington, D.C., n.d.

Islamic Center (Michigan City). *Islam in Michigan City, Past and Present*. Michigan City, Indiana, n.d.

Katibah, H. I. "Moslems of City Celebrating Pious Feast of Ramazan (sic.)." *Brooklyn Eagle*, April 18, 1925. In *The Arabs in America, 1492–1977 A Chronology and Fact Book*, p. 81. Edited by Beverlee Turner Mehdi. Dobbs Ferry, New York: Oceana Publications Inc., 1978.

Khan, Muhammad Zafrulla. *Ahmadiyyat The Renaissance of Islam*. London: Tabshir Publications, 1978.

Kritzeck, James and Winder, R. Bayly, eds. *The World of Islam*. New York: St. Martins Press, 1959.

LeBon, Gustave. *The World of Islamic Civilization*. Geneva: Tudor Publishing Company, 1974.

Levy, Ruben. *The Social Structure of Islam*. Cambridge: Cambridge University Press, 1957.

Lewis, Bernard, ed. *Islam and the Arab World: Faith, People, Culture*. New York: Alfred A. Knopf in association with American Heritage Publishing Company, Inc., 1976.

_____*Islam from the Prophet Muhammad to the Capture of Constantinople* 2 Vols. New York: Harper Torchbooks, 1974.

Lincoln, Charles Eric. *The Black Muslims in America*. Revised Edition. Boston: Beacon Press, 1973.

Little, Malcolm. *The Autobiography of Malcolm X*. New York: Grove Press, 1973.

MCC Bulletin. Published six times a year by the Muslim Community Center, Inc., Bethesda, Maryland.

Mehdi, Beverlee Turner, ed. *The Arabs in America, 1492–1977 A Chronology and Fact Book*. Dobbs Ferry, New York: Oceana Publications, Inc., 1978.

The Muslim Star. Published monthly by the Federation of Islamic Associations, Detroit, Michigan.

The Muslim World: A Quarterly Journal of Islamic Study and of Christian Interpretation Among Muslims. Published by the Hartford Seminary Foundation in Hartford, Connecticut.

Newsletter of the Task Force on Christian-Muslim Relations. A Project of the Commission on Faith and Order of the National Council of the Churches of Christ in the U.S.A. in Cooperation with the Duncan Black Macdonald Center for the Study of Islam and Christian-Muslim Relations, The Hartford Seminary Foundation. No. 8, April 1980.

Parish, James Robert and Stanke, Don D. *The Swashbucklers*. New Rochelle, New York: Arlington House, 1976.

Pear, Robert. "Capital Mosque Reflects Islam Turmoil." *New York Times*, August 24, 1980, p. 65.

Savory, R.M., ed. *Introduction to Islamic Civilization*. Cambridge: Cambridge University Press, 1976.

Shadid, Michael A. *Crusading Doctor*. Boston: Meador Publishing Company, 1956.

Shiloah, A. "The Dimension of Sound, Islamic Music-Philosophy, Theory and Practice." In *Islam and the Arab World: Faith, People, Culture*, pp. 161–180. Edited by Bernard Lewis. New York: Alfred A. Knopf in Association with American Heritage Publishing Company Inc., 1976.

Smith, Wilfred Cantwell. *Islam in Modern History*. Princeton: Princeton University Press, 1957.

Sullivan, Ronald. "A Moslem School Upsets Hunterdon." *New York Times*, May 21, 1978. sec. xi p. 20.

Sulzberger, A.O. Jr. "Roots of War in the Gulf." *New York Times*, September 24, 1980, sec. A, p. 10.

Sweet, Louise E. "Reconstituting a Lebanese Village Society in a Canadian City." In *Arabic Speaking Communities in American Cities*, Edited by Beverlee Turner Mehdi. New York: Oceana Publications, Inc., 1974, pp. 39 51.

Time. "The World of Islam." "Islam the Militant Revival." 113 No. 16, April 16, 1979, 40 ff.

Younis, Adele. "The Coming of the Arabic-Speaking People to the United States." Ph.D. dissertation, Boston University, 1961.

Watt, W. Montgomery. *The Formative Period of Islamic Thought.* Edinburgh: Edinburgh University Press, 1973.

Wigle, Laurel D. "An Arab Muslim Community in Michigan." In *Arabic Speaking Communities in American Cities,* pp. 155–167. Edited by Barbara C. Aswad. New York: Center for Migration Studies 1974.

Williams, John Alden, ed. *Islam.* New York: George Braziller, 1952.

Wolf, C. Umhau. "The Islamic Federation, 1952: 'Muslims in the American Mid-West,'" in *The Muslim World.* L (January 1960), 42–43. Quoted in *The Arabs in America 1492–1977 A Chronology and Fact Book,* p. 103. Edited by Beverlee Turner Mehdi. Dobbs Ferry, New York: Oceana Publications Inc., 1978.

Index